21st CENTURY LIVES
ENTREPRENEURS

Adam Sutherland

WAYLAND

First published in 2010 by Wayland

Copyright © Wayland 2010

Wayland
338 Euston Road
London NW1 3BH

Wayland Australia
Level 17/207 Kent Street
Sydney, NSW 2000

Senior editor: Camilla Lloyd
Designer: Steven Prosser
Picture researcher: Shelley Noronha

Picture Acknowledgments: The author and publisher would like to thank the following for allowing their pictures to be reproduced in this publication: Cover & 8: © Tony Avelar/Bloomberg/Getty Images; © Michael Grecco/Getty Images: 1 & 16; © Matt Stewart/Rex Features: 4; © Eammon McCormack/Wireimage/Getty Images: 5; © Ian Gavan/Getty Images: 6; © Richard Young/Rex Features: 7; © UPPA/Photoshot: 9, 17; © Francesco Guidicini/Rex Features: 10; © Topham/PA: 11; © Sipa Press/Rex Features: 12; © Craig Ruttle/AP/Press Association Images: 13; © PA Photos/TopFoto: 14; © Chris Jackson/Getty Images: 15; © Claire Greenway/Getty Images: 18; © Chris Bourchier/Rex Features: 19; © James D. Morgan/Rex Features: 20; © Steve Liss/Time & Life Pictures/Getty Images: 21.

British Library Cataloguing in Publication Data:
Sutherland, Adam.
    Entrepreneurs. -- (21st century lives)
    1. Businesspeople--Biography--Juvenile literature.
    2. Entrepreneurship--Juvenile literature.
    I. Title II. Series
    338'.04'0922-dc22

ISBN: 978 0 7502 6418 1

Printed in China

Wayland is a division of Hachette Children's Books, an Hachette UK company.

www.hachette.co.uk

Contents

Peter Jones

The dragon in the den

Peter Jones at the launch of his National Enterprise Academy in London, 2009.

> **"...Everyone's typecast me as the Simon Cowell of business... Cowell speaks his mind and so do I. If...the idea is ludicrous, I am not going to hold back."**
>
> **Peter Jones in**
> **The Sunday Times, 2005**

Name: Peter Jones CBE (Commander of the Order of the British Empire)

Date and place of birth: 18 March 1966 in Langley, near Slough, Berkshire

Education: Peter attended Windsor Boy's School and took A-levels in Economics, Biology and Geography.

Getting started: Peter was a keen tennis player, and at 16 he set up his first business – his own tennis academy. He launched a computer business in his early twenties, making and selling own-brand personal computers (PCs). The business was extremely successful but had to close when a customer went under owing Peter a lot of money.

Making it big: Peter spent 12 months working for Phones 4 U and then in 1998 set up a direct competitor company, Phones International Group. The company made £14 million at the end of the first year, £44 million by the end of the second, and over £150 million by 2006.

Awards and achievements: As one of the original dragons on *Dragon's Den*, Peter has become very well known to the public. *Dragon's Den* is a TV programme that sees entrepreneurs pitch for investment from Britain's most successful businessmen and women. Peter also launched his own highly successful show, *American Inventor*, in the USA with the help of Simon Cowell. He was awarded a CBE in the 2009 New Year's Honours List for services to business, entrepreneurship and young people.

Secret to success: Peter has always loved business. He is extremely competitive, and trusts his own judgement, backing good ideas with investment.

Something you might not know about him: Peter is 6 feet 7 inches tall – the same height as England footballer Peter Crouch.

The team, including Peter (far right) launch *Dragon's Den: From Pitch to Profit* in 2007. There are three more titles to be released in 2010.

Peter Jones is the longest-running Dragon on the BBC's hit business entertainment show *Dragon's Den*. He is always on the lookout for great ideas – however crazy they might sound at first – and doesn't mind telling people if their inventions and business plans simply don't make sense. He's also willing to take a chance. Among other things, he has invested in a fashion magazine, a jerk chicken sauce, a pop band, a sculptor, and a teddy bear with an MP3 player in its tummy that became the UK's second best-selling toy!

As a child, Peter would sit at his father's desk in the leather swivel chair, daydreaming about running the company. He left school at 16 and turned his tennis abilities (he was a county-standard player) to good use, by launching a tennis academy. But it's been in computing and telecommunications where Peter has really made his mark. He built his first fortune selling own-brand PCs but lost everything when a company went bust owing him lots of money. He sold his house and his Porsche and moved back home with his parents.

Peter then joined computer company Siemens Nixdorf as their youngest ever Head of PC Business. But he was always looking for the next move, and after 12 months working for Phones 4 U, he set up a direct rival, Phones International Group. Peter worked around the clock, often sleeping on the office floor, to make the business a success. The company became one of the fastest growing businesses in Europe, and made Peter a very rich man.

The success of *Dragon's Den* has helped Peter and his fellow Dragons become extremely recognisable faces. It has also helped make business seem exciting and interesting to a younger audience. Peter feels very strongly that schools should encourage the entrepreneurial spirit in teenagers, and has invested £5 million of his own money to launch a series of National Enterprise Academies around the country where 16 to 19 year olds will be taught the skills necessary to launch their own companies. This is one Dragon who's not so scary after all.

"One of [Peter's] top tips is never use the word 'failure' in relation to your career. [He] always substitutes the word 'feedback' for 'failure'."

Alison Roberts in the *Evening Standard*, 2008

Sir Philip Green

King of the high street

Sir Philip's store makes up 12 per cent of the UK retail clothing market.

❝Part of the art of being entrepreneurial... is having vision. Things turn up, and you're able to react or respond to them... Good ideas are only good ideas if you can execute them and turn them into something real.❞

Sir Philip to the *Independent*, 2007

Name: Sir Philip Green

Date and place of birth: 14 March 1952 in Croydon, South London

Education: Sir Philip went to Carmel College boarding school in Oxfordshire from the age of eight, and left school at 15 after taking his GCSEs.

Getting started: His first job was working for a shoe importer. Sir Philip planned to learn everything about the retail business before setting up on his own. In the early 1970s, he started his first business, borrowing £20,000 from the bank and selling imported jeans from the Far East to retailers in London.

Making it big: Sir Philip specialises in buying failing or underperforming companies and turning their finances around. In 1995 he bought sports retailer Olympus for £1 (and £30 million worth of debt) and sold it three years later for £550 million. In 1999, Sir Philip bought BHS (British Home Stores) for £200 million, and has tripled the profits to £200 million per year. In 2002 he bought the Arcadia Group (including Topshop, Topman, Miss Selfridge, Wallis and others). The group has become very successful, and currently makes around £380 million profit per year.

Awards and achievements: Sir Philip was knighted on 17 June 2006. The stores he owns account for 12 per cent of the UK clothing retail market, making his clothes business second only to Marks and Spencer.

Secret to success: Sir Philip had an entrepreneurial spirit from an early age. He sees opportunities and is not afraid to take risks in order to make money.

Something you might not know about him: He lives in the Dorchester hotel during the week, and travels to Monaco by private jet at the weekends to see his wife and children.

The ability to spot an opportunity and act on it quickly has made Sir Philip Green a billionaire. He has a sixth sense for retail, knows what customers want, and knows when companies aren't delivering it. Every week he walks the length of Oxford Street, one of London's busiest shopping streets, with his staff, looking in shop windows – his own included – and deciding what they're doing right, what they're doing wrong and making changes accordingly.

Sir Philip's love of retail started at an early age. At 12, he was working for a shoe importer, earning £20 per week. He came up with the idea of matching up stray single shoes and selling them as pairs, and increased his earnings to £150 in one weekend!

Bitten by the business bug, Sir Philip left school at 15 and threw himself into the world of work. He made his first million buying an unsuccessful jeans retailer called Jean Jeannie in the 1970s, turning round its fortunes and then selling it on to Lee Cooper. He did the same thing with Olympus Sports and Sears department stores, before buying – and so far keeping – BHS and the Arcadia Group.

One of Sir Philip's most memorable recent deals has been hiring British supermodel Kate Moss to design a regular collection for Topshop. Kate's designs have been a huge success for the store, in terms of sales and press headlines.

The model, who calls him 'Uncle Phil', is also rumoured to have been offered the job of worldwide style director for Sir Philip's new business venture with his close friend Simon Cowell. The pair have formed a company called Greenwell Entertainment that the two

Sir Philip, Kate Moss and Simon Cowell at the Beth Ditto for Evans launch party in 2009.

men say will be 'as big as Disney'. It is believed that Greenwell will be in the business of creating hit worldwide television shows, and producing and selling merchandise for those shows through Sir Philip's chain of retail stores. Whatever the future holds for Sir Philip, it's bound to be a huge success.

"Philip is a shrewd businessman. He's great fun. He enjoys life to the full, he's energetic and he's curious."

Sir Stuart Rose, chairman of Marks and Spencer, 2009

Steve Jobs

The man behind Mac

Steve Jobs shows the world the iPad – Apple's new world-changing invention.

> **❝ My model for business is the Beatles. They were four guys [who] balanced each other. And the total was greater than the sum of the parts. Great things in business are not done by one person, they are done by a team of people. ❞**
>
> **On the *60 Minutes* TV show, 2008**

Name: Steven Paul 'Steve' Jobs

Date and place of birth: 24 February 1955 in San Francisco, United States

Education: Steve was adopted at birth and grew up in Mountain View, Santa Clara County, California. Steve attended Homestead High School in Cupertino, California and often attended after-school lectures at the Hewlett-Packard computer company in Palo Alto, who gave him his first summer job.

Getting started: Steve's first job was as a technician for the games company Atari. He worked on a computer game called Breakout, and with colleague Steve Wozniak, radically improved the performance of the game, making a £3,250 ($5,000) bonus.

Making it big: Steve co-founded Apple in 1976. The company produced high-quality, innovative computers, and Steve was worth £130 million ($200 million) by the age of 25. In 1985 he was forced to resign from Apple after a fall-out with fellow directors, and bought Pixar, the computer animation company. Pixar made a deal with Disney to co-finance and distribute their films, and have since won several Best Animated Feature awards at the Oscars. In 1996, Steve returned to Apple, and has made the company a huge success, launching the iMac, the iPod, iTunes store and most recently the iPhone and iPad.

Awards and achievements: Steve was awarded the National Medal for Technology in 1985. In 2007, he was named the most powerful person in business by *Fortune* magazine. In 2009, Steve was selected as the most admired entrepreneur among teenagers.

Secret to success: Steve believes in the ability of technology to improve and enhance people's lives. Every Apple product is made with that in mind.

Something you might not know about him: Steve is famous for always wearing the same outfit – black long-sleeved turtleneck jumper, Levi's jeans and New Balance trainers!

Steve Jobs is the head of the most admired and innovative technology company in the world. Apple's success is based on Steve's belief in the importance of functionality and product design, and an ability to spot and develop 'the next big thing'. Apple has changed computers from boring grey boxes to exciting, well-designed products. They have changed the way people listen to music by inventing the iPod, the world's most successful digital music player, and they are set to do the same with books and publishing with the invention of the iPad.

Steve founded Apple in 1976 with friends Steve Wozniak and Ronald Wayne. Steve had an amazing drive to be the best – he hired the most innovative computer programmers from around the industry and inspired them to do their greatest work. But his ambition made him difficult to work with, and not a good team player. After one fall out too many, he was forced out of Apple in 1985.

His shares in Apple had already made him a multi-millionaire, but Steve was determined to keep driving innovation in the industry, and his next move was to buy a computer animation company called The Graphics Group from *Star Wars* director George Lucas. The company, which was later renamed Pixar, cost £6.6 million ($10 million). Steve signed an important contract with Disney to co-produce animated films, and since then Pixar has made hits including *Toy Story* (1995), *Finding Nemo* (2003), *The Incredibles* and most recently *Up* (2009). In 2006, Disney bought Pixar for a massive £4.8 billion ($7.4 billion) and Steve became Disney's biggest single shareholder, with 7 per cent of the company's stock.

When Apple bought Steve's company NeXt Computers in 1996, he returned to the company he founded. At this time, Apple was in financial trouble, and Steve helped turn its fortunes around, launching new must-have products like the iMac personal computer, and the iPod MP3 player and iTunes store. Steve and Apple have innovated every aspect of the entertainment industry – from home computers, to film, music and now books.

Steve Jobs' presentations are big showbiz events. Here he launches the iTunes store in Europe in 2004.

"Jobs has become a global cultural guru, shaping what entertainment we watch, how we listen to music, and what sort of objects we use to work and play. He has changed the game for entire industries."

Fortune magazine, 2008

Martha Lane Fox
The first lady of the Internet

Martha at Lastminute.com headquarters in 2005. Her image was part of the brand's success.

" Nine to five, that's just not the way I work. I am happy to work all the time if it's something I am passionate about. **"**

Martha Lane Fox to Sarah Cassidy, the *Independent*, 2010

Name: Martha Lane Fox

Date and place of birth: 10 February 1973 in Oxford

Education: Martha attended Westminster School in London, and then Magdalen College, Oxford, where she studied ancient and modern history. Her father, Robin, is a classical history professor at the same university.

Getting started: Her first job after university was for a consulting firm, Spectrum, which was involved in information technology (IT). The first project she worked on was for British Telecom, called 'What is the Internet?'

Making it big: At Spectrum, Martha met Brent Hoberman, and in 1998 the pair founded Lastminute.com, an online travel and gift business. The business became one of the best known companies of the UK Internet boom, and when it 'floated' on the stock market in March 2000, it was valued as high as £733 million. Floating a company means allowing the public to buy shares. These shares can then be traded on the stock market. Martha stepped down from the business in December 2003, but remained a shareholder until Lastminute.com was sold in 2005. She made £13.5 million from the sale.

Awards and achievements: In 2009, Martha was appointed the Government's Digital Inclusion Champion, with the responsibility of getting an additional four million people online by 2012.

Secret to success: Martha is extremely hard working (she worked 18-hour days at Lastminute.com) and a very good motivator of people. She understood that the 'value' of Lastminute.com was related to how well-known she became. The share prices that the company achieved are often put down to 'Martha-mania'!

Something you might not know about her: Martha had a bad car accident in Morocco in 2004, and broke her right arm, her pelvis and her right leg. She still walks with a stick.

Martha and fellow Lastminute.com founder Brent Hoberman.

However many other companies she launches, and however many more millions she makes, Martha Lane Fox will always be known as the woman behind Lastminute.com. She was an icon of Britain's first 'dotcom' boom, and her visibility, her PR skills and her undoubted talent with people, helped make Lastminute.com the success it is today.

Martha founded Lastminute.com, an online travel and gift business, in 1998. She and fellow founder Brent Hoberman ran the company, with Martha as Managing Director and Brent as CEO (Chief Executive Officer). The pair floated Lastminute.com on the stock exchange in 2000, with share prices reaching as high as 487^{1}/2p per share on the second day of trading, valuing the company at £733 million.

Over the next 18 months, the value of the company sank to £32 million, but when Martha eventually stepped down as Managing Director at the end of December 2003, the share price had recovered to 222^{1}/2p, valuing the company at £667 million.

When Lastminute.com was eventually sold to one of its biggest rivals, Travelocity, in 2005, Martha made £13 million from the sale. However, she had no intention of sitting back and taking things easy. Instead, she threw herself back into new businesses and new challenges. In 2005, she launched a Tokyo-style private karaoke bar in London called Lucky Voice. The company now have five bars around the country, and have launched a Lucky Voice Party Box to be used on home computers.

Martha suffered a very bad car accident while on holiday in Morocco in 2004, and spent several years recuperating. Now back to full fitness (although she still walks with a stick), Martha continues to be as hard working and motivated to succeed and share her experience as ever.

She is on the board of directors of Channel 4, and is a non-executive director of Marks and Spencer. In June 2009, she was appointed as the Government's Digital Inclusion Champion, with a two-year mission to increase the number of people going online – particularly among the elderly and the less advantaged. Martha approaches everything she does with enthusiasm, and a will to win.

"Martha has been a fantastic asset [to Lastminute.com]... Her popularity with the press was always fantastic for the brand. She's an aspirational figure, people want to be like her."

Brent Hoberman to *The Times*, 2003

Mark Zuckerberg
The face of Facebook

Mark in 2008 after the announcement that he had become the world's youngest billionaire.

" **When I started Facebook... [I] believed that people being able to share the information they wanted and having access to the information they wanted is just a better world.** "

Mark Zuckerberg to
Wired **magazine, 2009**

Name: Mark Elliot Zuckerberg

Date and place of birth: 14 May 1984 in White Plains, New York, USA, the son of a dentist father and a psychiatrist mother

Education: Mark attended Ardsley High School, and then Phillips Exeter Academy where he started developing computer programmes. Mark built a music player that used artificial intelligence to learn the user's listening habits. Microsoft and AOL both tried to hire Mark as a programmer but he decided to attend the prestigious Harvard University instead.

Getting started: Mark launched Facebook on 4 February 2004. The idea came from his time at Phillips Exeter Academy which, like most colleges, published an annual student directory known as the 'Facebook'. Mark's invention was initially for Harvard students only, but then expanded to fellow universities Stanford, Dartmouth, Columbia, Cornell and Yale.

Making it big: During the 2004 summer holidays, Mark moved to Palo Alto, California with Harvard roommate Dustin Moskovitz. Facebook found its first investors, and has since grown from strength to strength. In October 2007, Microsoft paid £157 million ($240 million) for just 1.6 per cent in the company, making it worth £10 billion ($15 billion) at the time of sale.

Awards and achievements: As of January 2010, Mark is the youngest self-made businessman worth more than £65 million (one billion dollars).

Secret to success: Mark took a simple idea, and created something that has changed the way the world communicates. He always focuses on what will improve Facebook and is constantly improving and updating it.

Something you might not know about him: A film based on Mark and his fellow Facebook founders was filmed in 2010 starring Justin Timberlake and directed by David Fincher (the director of *The Curious Case of Benjamin Button*).

Mark's ambition was to change the way the world communicates. With Facebook, he achieved it.

Facebook has helped Mark Zuckerberg become a billionaire. But the first version he launched, earned him nothing more than a severe telling off from his Harvard college professors and caused an uproar on campus!

Mark wanted to create an online university directory, listing all students and staff. Harvard kept giving him reasons why it was impossible. So one night, Mark hacked into the student records and launched a simple website called Facemash, containing student photos and information. Four hours, 450 visitors and 22,000 photo views later, Harvard pulled the plug on his Internet connection, and reprimanded him for the unauthorised use of student data.

Mark remained convinced that the demand was there for the sharing of information, and easy, open communication. So he persevered with the idea. First, he persuaded Harvard to allow him to launch an 'official' version of Facebook to serve the university's students and lecturers. Then he expanded it to fellow universities Stanford, Dartmouth, Columbia, Cornell and Yale.

Enlisting help from his roommate Dustin Moskovitz (Facebook co-founder and vice president of engineering), and old school friend Adam D'Angelo (chief technology officer), Mark spent the summer holidays at the end of his second year in Palo Alto,

California, the home of the world's most influential hi-tech companies, looking for investors to back his new business.

With investors' money in the bank, the company found its first offices and gradually expanded Facebook into all the US colleges, high schools, companies, and eventually worldwide. The company consistently doubled in size every six months, and by the end of 2009 had reached a massive 350 million users worldwide.

Mark and his co-founders have turned down all offers to sell Facebook. Yahoo reportedly offered £65 million ($1 billion) in 2007, but they did sell a small 1.6 per cent of the company to Microsoft. Facebook continues to develop, allowing outside programmers to design Apps (applications) and platforms that will make the service better. Mark believed that the world wants to communicate, and he's been proved right.

"[Mark's] life so far is like a movie script. A supersmart kid invents a tech phenomenon... and launches it to rave reviews... Just three years in, what started as a networking site for college students has become a go-to tool for [350] million registered users."

Ellen McGirt, www.fastcompany.com, 2007

Karren Brady
The football manager

Karren was a prominent and popular figure at Birmingham City Football Club.

> **"Every day is difficult if you're running a team of people. You've got to be enthusiastic and strategic every day... I [love] the challenge of it."**
>
> **Karren Brady in the *Guardian*, 2008**

Name: Karren Brady

Date and place of birth: 4 April 1969 in Edmonton, North London

Education: Karren went to Poles Convent, a boarding school in Ware, Hertfordshire and then to Aldenham School, Elstree for her A-levels.

Getting started: Karren's first job at 18 was for advertising agency Saatchi and Saatchi. She left there to join LBC radio where she sold advertising space for the 4-5am Asian Hour show. One of her first clients was publisher David Sullivan, and Karren persuaded him to spend £2 million in advertising in just six months. Sullivan was so impressed, he offered her a job, and Karren became one of the company's directors at just 20 years old.

Making it big: Sullivan and business partner David Gold bought Birmingham City Football Club in March 1993, and made 23-year-old Karren the Managing Director. She became the youngest Managing Director of a UK public limited company when the club offered shares to the public in 1997. Karren left Birmingham when new owners took over in October 2009, but was soon appointed Vice-Chairman of West Ham United, when it was bought by Sullivan and Gold.

Awards and achievements: Karren was named Business Woman of the Year 2007. As well as being Vice-Chairman of West Ham United FC, she is currently Chairman of Kerrang! Radio, Non-Executive Director of Sport England, and was until recently a board member of England's 2018 World Cup bid.

Secret to success: One of Karren's big talents is employing talented members of staff, and giving them the confidence to do a great job.

Something you might not know about her: Karren is married to ex-footballer Paul Peschisolido. She sold him twice when he played for Birmingham City.

Karren Brady speaking at a meeting of interntional business leaders in November 2007.

Karren Brady is Britain's favourite businesswoman. Clever, funny and completely unflappable, Karren has become famous as a woman running the most male of companies – a football club.

Karren has been driven and super-ambitious from an early age. At seven years old she had a poster in her bedroom window offering manicures and pedicures. She completed her A-levels, then immediately started work at prestigious advertising agency Saatchi and Saatchi. She quickly moved to LBC radio, and met millionaire publisher David Sullivan when she spent five hours in his office waiting room, before twisting his arm to buy £2 million worth of advertising space on a radio show in the middle of the night with a handful of listeners. Amazingly, his newspaper sales went up, and Sullivan offered Karren a job as his sales and marketing manager.

Then Karren spotted an advert in the *Financial Times* for Birmingham City Football Club, and advised Sullivan to buy it. The deal was done in March 1993, and Sullivan and co-owner David Gold made Karren their managing director at just 23 years old.

At a time when many football club boardrooms didn't allow women, Karren braved criticism from the sports press, and even occasional abuse from the players, and quickly turned Birmingham City – then in the old Second Division – into a financial success. Within a year she had helped the football club make a profit for the first time in its 131-year history. And when Birmingham was floated on the stock exchange in 1997, it was valued at £25 million. She also helped the club win promotion to the Premiership where they are still flying high.

Karren is now vice-chairman of West Ham United, and Alan Sugar's new second-in-command on the sixth series of BBC1's *The Apprentice*. She previously helped out as a guest interviewer in series four and five, and was also the winning captain for *Comic Relief Does The Apprentice* in 2007, raising £1 million for Comic Relief. Karren is an inspiration for any budding businesswoman.

"Brady comes across as a natural successor to Sir Alan Sugar, if he ever gave up his seat at the head of the TV boardroom. She certainly has the patter and the mindset."

In the *Guardian*, 2008

Larry Page and Sergey Brin
The men behind Google

Larry (left) and Sergey get dressed for a day in the office in 2002 – Google style!

❝ From a very early age I realised I wanted to invent things. So I became really interested in technology... and business. So probably from when I was 12 I knew I was going to start a company eventually. ❞

Larry Page, 2008

Names: Lawrence 'Larry' Page and Sergey Mikhailovich Brin

Dates and places of birth: Larry: 26 March 1973 in Lansing, Michigan, USA; Sergey: 21 August 1973 in Moscow, Russia

Education: Larry earned a Bachelor of Science degree in computer engineering from the University of Michigan. Sergey did a Bachelor of Science degree at the University of Maryland. The two men met in 1995 studying for their Ph.Ds at Stanford University. (Ph.D stands for Doctor of Philosophy. It is the highest degree someone can achieve.)

Getting started: When Larry was studying for his Ph.D, the Internet contained an estimated 10 million documents, with a countless number of links between them. Larry and Sergey decided to solve the problem of how to rank these documents from most relevant to least relevant, depending on what information a person was trying to find.

Making it big: In August 1996 the first version of Google was made available on the Stanford University website. The pair quickly discovered they had created a groundbreaking new search engine and put their studies on hold. In 1998, they founded Google Inc, setting up in a garage with £65,000 ($100,000) investment.

Awards and achievements: In 2004, Larry and Sergey received the Marconi Foundation Prize, the highest award in engineering, and in 2005 were elected Fellows of the American Academy of Arts and Sciences. They are currently ranked joint 26th of the world's billionaires, and are joint 5th richest men in America.

Secret to success: Both men have an unstoppable desire to improve the way we use technology, and a belief that technology can improve our lives.

Something you might not know about them: At university, Larry built an inkjet printer out of Lego bricks.

Larry and Sergey are both classic 'computer geeks'. Larry's mum and dad were both computer science professors, Sergey's dad was a mathematics professor and his mum was a research scientist at NASA's Goddard Space Flight Centre.

The pair's revolutionary search engine was originally called 'Backrub', the nickname of Larry's Ph.D project. The name was eventually changed to Google, originating from a misspelling of the word 'googol' – the number 1 followed by one hundred zeros – which was meant to signify the amount of information that Google was able to handle!

Google makes 99 per cent of its income from advertising on its search engine. However, the company has more recently launched a number of additional services, including its own email service Googlemail, Google Books (a book search engine), Google Maps for navigation, You Tube (bought for $1.65 billion or £1 billion), Google Earth (photography from around the planet), Google Translate (an online translation tool)

The Google founders, Sergey (left) and Larry, want to organise all the world's information.

Google is the Internet's most visited website. The search engine is used by over 90 per cent of UK Internet visitors, runs over one million computers in centres around the world, and processes over one billion search requests every day.

Thanks to Google's AdWords programme, which charges advertisers a fee for every 'click' through to their websites, Google's founders Larry Page and Sergey Brin are both billionaires, and the site's online adverts account for 40 per cent of all the advertising dollars spent online.

So how did Google get to be so big so fast? Put simply, it took the process of searching for information on the Internet, and made it faster, generating better, more accurate results than any of its competitors.

and Android, an operation system for mobile phones.

Some of the company's work, particularly Google Books and Google Earth have raised concerns about personal privacy and ownership of content. But Google claim their aim has always been 'to organise the world's information and make it universally accessible and useful'. They have certainly achieved their ambitions.

"We don't have a five-year plan, we don't have a two-year plan, we don't have a one-year plan. We have a mission and a strategy, and the mission is... to organise all the world's information. And the strategy is to do it through innovation."

Eric Schmidt, Google CEO to *Wired* magazine, 2009

Lord Alan Sugar
The big name in British business

Lord Alan Sugar has become famous for the catchphrase 'Your fired!'

Name: Lord Alan Michael Sugar

Date and place of birth: 24 March 1947 in Hackney, East London

Education: Lord Sugar attended Brooke House School in Upper Clapton, but left school at 16 to start his own business.

Getting started: The youngest of four children, Lord Sugar lived with his parents in a council flat. His father, Nathan, worked as a tailor in the East End clothing industry. While he was still at school, Lord Sugar earned money by boiling beetroots for the local greengrocer. His first job was selling car aerials out of the back of a van having invested £100 (his life savings) on stock. By the time he got married at 21, he could afford a house and a car.

Making it big: Lord Sugar's business empire was built on Amstrad (short for Alan Michael Sugar Trading), a consumer electronic business he started in 1968. Throughout the 1970s and 1980s, Amstrad specialised in car stereos, TVs and hi-fis. The company moved into personal computers, games consoles, and finally satellite set-top boxes. The company was sold to Sky in 2007 for £125 million.

Awards and achievements: Lord Sugar was knighted in 2000 for his services to business. In 2009, he was awarded a peerage by former Prime Minister Gordon Brown and became Lord Sugar of Clapton.

Secret to success: Despite his success, Lord Sugar is still ambitious and always wants to be the best at what he does. Amstrad spotted a trend, and supplied products that people wanted at the right price.

Something you might not know about him: Lord Sugar owns a £360,000 Rolls-Royce Phantom with the number plate AMS1.

Lord Alan Sugar is one of Britain's best known and most successful businessmen. He is worth an estimated £700 million and has been in the public eye for over 20 years. For ten years, from June 1991, he was the outspoken chairman of Tottenham Hotspur Football Club. He saved the club from bankruptcy, but was never a favourite with the fans, who thought he didn't do enough to 'buy success' for the team. He fell out with players and managers during his time in charge and eventually sold his shares in the club for around £50 million.

Lord Sugar in front of the Rolls-Royce Phantom that carries his initials, AMS1.

Since 2005 he has been the hard-to-please boss on BBC's hit business reality show *The Apprentice*. Every series, fourteen hopeful candidates compete for the chance of a job with Lord Sugar. Instead, all but one of them gets to hear Lord Sugar point the finger and say, 'You're fired!'

The winner of each series finds him or herself working in one of Lord Sugar's companies, which today include Amsprop (property), Viglen (information technology), Amscreen (advertising) and Amsair (business and executive jet charters).

Lord Sugar's fortune was built in the home electronics industry. Amstrad found success by using cheap and efficient production methods to provide affordable home hi-fi equipment, and then home computers. During the 1980s, Amstrad was so successful that it doubled its profits and company value every year, and at its peak was valued at £1.2 billion.

During the 1990s, Lord Sugar diversified production, and among other things released a games console, an early version of the Smartphone, and a combined home phone and emailer before winning the contract

to produce Sky set-top boxes. He eventually sold Amstrad to BSkyB in 2007, and stepped down as Chairman in 2008.

Lord Sugar's most successful business today is his property company. He owns around £300 million worth of commercial property (used for offices) all over the UK – from warehouses in Essex, to huge upmarket developments in some of London's most expensive areas, like the City of London and Mayfair.

Most recently, he was recruited by former Prime Minister Gordon Brown's Labour government to offer advice and feedback on business and the economy. He is one of the richest businessmen in Britain and Lord Sugar isn't showing any signs of slowing down just yet.

"[Lord Sugar]... wants to make us all more confident. If you naturally defer to others, apologise for your success or don't really believe you can make it, you are your own number-one obstacle."

In the *Evening Standard*, 2008

Ben and Jerry
The ice cream men

Name: Ben Cohen and Jerry Greenfield

Dates and places of birth: Ben: 18 March 1951 in Brooklyn, New York, USA; Jerry: 14 March 1951 in Brooklyn, New York, USA

Education: Ben and Jerry met at Merrick Avenue Junior High School in 1963. They both attended Calhoun High School before heading off to separate universities.

Getting started: After university, Ben worked as a McDonald's cashier, a security guard and a taxi driver, and Jerry worked as a lab technician, having failed to get into medical school. The two men took a $5 (£3.20) correspondence course (course where study is not carried out at a university, but through mail correspondence) in ice cream making and decided to open their own ice cream parlour.

Making it big: The pair set up their first Ben & Jerry's shop in Burlington, Vermont in 1978, and made their ice cream with fresh local milk and cream. Because Ben suffered from anosmia – a loss of smell and near loss of taste – they also added larger than usual chunks of cookies, brownies and so on to their ice cream to satisfy Ben's need for food with texture. The company has since opened around 200 shops and has annual earnings of £155 million ($240 million).

Awards and achievements: The two men were named US Small Businessmen of the Year in 1988. Ben & Jerry's was sold to the Unilever company in 2000, but the pair still remain active in the company.

Secret to success: Ben & Jerry's made ice cream fun. They found a quirky, local, 'green' niche and worked hard to compete against the giant companies.

Something you might not know about them: Ben and Jerry were going to open a bagel shop, but eventually chose ice cream because the equipment was much cheaper!

Ben (left) and Jerry open their first shop in Australia in November 2009.

❝Nobody's going to buy ice cream that they don't like, just because they believe in the social values of the company. But it certainly has given the product, the brand, a pointed difference, and... made people feel good about it.❞

Ben Cohen to the *Boston Phoenix*, 2008

Ben (left) and Jerry have made ice cream fun. They also give money to charity and care for the environment.

Chunky Monkey, Cherry Garcia, Phish Food, Jamaican Me Crazy. Ben Cohen and Jerry Greenfield don't just make delicious ice cream, they make *fun* ice cream. Add to that their homemade-looking packaging, their insistence on using locally sourced fresh milk and cream, and their outspoken support for green and humanitarian causes, and Ben & Jerry's is a fun and feelgood ice cream. A winning formula!

The two men met at junior high school at 12 years old. The story is that they met when they were both at the back of a cross-country run and being shouted at by a PE teacher to pick up the pace. Ben and Jerry are not classic entrepreneurs. In fact they both tried their hands at a number of different careers before deciding to open their first ice cream parlour.

The search for the best location – a warm weather college town (because students like to eat ice cream!) – led them to Burlington, Vermont, home of the University of Vermont. They opened their first shop on 5 May 1978 with £5,200 ($8,000) savings and a £2,600 ($4,000) bank loan, in a renovated petrol station. The following year, they marked their one-year anniversary by holding their first ever Free Cone Day, which is now a nationwide celebration giving away one million free cones every year.

The ice cream parlour was a huge success during the summer months, but was quiet in the winter, so they started selling to restaurants, firstly across Vermont, and eventually across the country. As the company began to grow and become more and more successful, the pair set up the Ben & Jerry's Foundation, which receives 7.5 per cent of the company's pre-tax profits, and supports thousands of good causes, including education, healthcare and the plight of refugees.

It's this charitable spirit, as much as the great flavours, that makes Ben & Jerry's such a popular brand. They were the first brand-name ice cream to be taken into space – on board the Space Shuttle. The company even renamed a flavour – Yes Pecan – in honour of US President Obama's election campaign slogan 'Yes We Can!' Although Ben and Jerry no longer own the company they founded, they remain just as involved and committed as ever.

"Whoever coined the phrase "nice guys finish last" obviously never met Ben Cohen and Jerry Greenfield... They found a way to combine profitability with social responsibility... and built one of the largest ice cream empires in the world."

www.entrepreneur.com, 2010

Other Entrepreneurs

Theo Paphitis

Born in Limassol, Cyprus, on 24 September 1959, Theodore 'Theo' Paphitis is well known for his appearances on hit BBC business show *Dragon's Den*. Theo moved to England with his parents when he was six, and attended the local comprehensive school. He showed an early flair for making money, running the school tuck shop at 15.

Theo has made a habit of spotting 'the next big thing' and acting on it quickly and successfully. By 23, he had set up his own property finance company, and made money from the rising value of commercial properties. He next spotted the emergence of mobile phones, and bought into a company called NAG Telecom. He did a deal with Ryman's to put NAG phones into every one of their stationery stores. When Ryman's got into financial trouble, Theo bought the company and turned it into a huge success, paying suppliers on time, and motivating store managers and staff.

Theo now owns Contessa, Partners, and co-owns Red Letter Days with fellow Dragon Peter Jones (pages 4 and 5). He recently sold his share in lingerie retailer La Senza for a reported £100 million.

Richard Reed

Richard Reed (born 13 February 1973) is one of the co-founders of Innocent Drinks. Innocent is a UK-based company with a 75 per cent share of the UK's smoothie market, which is currently worth £169 million per year. The company sells a massive two million smoothies per week and has been on *The Sunday Times* list of the fastest growing private companies for five years running.

Richard started the business with two college friends, Adam Balon and Jon Wright. The three of them spent £500 on fruit and set up a stall selling smoothies at a London music festival in 1998. Buyers were asked if the trio should give up their jobs and make smoothies full time, and to drop their empty cups in a 'Yes' bin or a 'No' bin. At the end of the festival, the 'Yes' bin was full, and there were only three cups in the 'No' bin. All three men resigned from their jobs the next day.

Innocent is well respected for its ethical and 'green' approach to business. Bottles are made from 50 per cent recycled plastic, fruit growers are paid premium rates, and the company's CO_2 emissions are offset every month to make it carbon neutral. Innocent drinks make you feel good inside and out!

Chad Hurley

The co-founder and Chief Executive Officer (CEO) of video sharing website YouTube was born in 1976 in Birdsboro, Pennsylvania, USA. Chad Meredith Hurley graduated from Indiana University of Pennsylvania in 1999, switching from computer science to graphic design mid-course. One of Chad's first jobs was with PayPal, the worldwide Internet payment service. For his first job interview he designed a logo that the company used for several years.

When eBay bought PayPal in 2002, Chad and colleagues Steve Chen and Jawed Karim left to set up YouTube. The site was their solution to the problem of how to distribute videos online. They couldn't send video files by email as the files were too large, and posting them online was time-consuming and difficult. On YouTube, users can post videos quickly and easily, and members can even set up their own 'channels'.

YouTube quickly became one of the most visited sites on the Internet. Ten hours of video are uploaded every minute, and hundreds of millions of videos are viewed every day. In October 2006 Google bought the site for £1 billion ($1.65 billion), turning Chad and his partners into instant multimillionaires. Nevertheless, Chad continues to run YouTube, and plans to help it keep growing into one of the world's most recognisable and used brands.

Russell Simmons

Music, television and fashion producer Russell Wendell Simmons (born 4 October 1957 in Queens, New York, USA) is a one-man trend-setting industry. In the late 1970s and early 1980s, Russell left his studies at City College in New York to pursue a career as a record producer, promoter and band manager. His work with bands including groundbreaking rap act Run DMC (featuring his brother Joseph) brought hip hop music into the mainstream.

Russell co-founded the record label Def Jam with record producer Rick Rubin, and guided the careers of bands and artists including the Beastie Boys, Public Enemy and LL Cool J. He then built on Def Jam's worldwide success to expand his business interests into clothing (Phat Farm, Argyleculture and American Classics), training shoes (Run Athletics), movie production, TV shows (Def Comedy Jam), magazines and even an advertising agency.

In 1999 Russell sold his stake in Def Jam to Universal Music for £65 million ($100 million) and is now believed to be the fourth richest man in hip hop, with a £220 million ($340 million) fortune. Only musicians Jay-Z, 50 Cent and Sean Combs are wealthier.

Sir Stelios Haji-Ioannou

Sir Stelios Haji-Ioannou (born 14 February 1967 in Athens, Greece) is best known for setting up the low-cost airline easyJet in 1995. He is an economics graduate from the London School of Economics, with a Masters (higher) degree in Shipping, Trade and Finance from Cass Business School at City University, London.

Sir Stelios's first job in 1988 was working for his father's shipping company. He did such a good job that four years later, at just 25, he negotiated a £19 million ($30 million) payout from his dad, and set up his own shipping company, which he floated on the New York stock market and eventually sold for £840 million ($1.3 billion).

Sir Stelios is a serial entrepreneur who built on the success of easyJet to build an 'easy empire', which now includes easyInternetcafe, easyHotel, easyBus, easyCar and easyCruise. In June 2006 Stelios received a knighthood from the Queen for services to entrepreneurship. Most recently, he has set up the Stelios Philanthropic Foundation to provide support and financial help to new businesses, higher education and environmental causes.

Oprah Winfrey

Talk show host, actress and businesswoman, Orpah Gail 'Oprah' Winfrey was born on 29 January 1954 in Kosciusko, Mississippi, USA. Oprah is best known for her multi-award winning talk show, *Oprah*, which is the most popular show of its kind in history.

Born in to poverty to a teenage single mother in Mississippi, Oprah lived with her grandmother until she was 6, before moving to Milwaukee to live with her mother. At 14, she went to live with her father in Nashville, Tennessee, and won a scholarship to Tennessee State University where she studied communication. She started reading the local evening news while still in her teens, and soon got transferred to a daytime talk show slot. She quickly boosted the show's ratings from third place to first place, and then decided to branch out on her own, launching her own television production company and broadcasting her show around the world.

A millionaire by the age of 32, Oprah has produced and starred in several films, has co-authored five books, and publishes two magazines, *O, The Oprah Magazine* and *O at Home*. She was ranked the richest African American of the 20th century, with an annual salary of around £195 million ($300 million), and was the world's first black billionaire.

Index

21st Century Lives

Contents of books in the series: